DATE DUE

GAYLORD	PRINTED IN U.S.A

RELIGIONS OF THE WORLD

I Am Muslim

❧ JESSICA CHALFONTE ❧

The Rosen Publishing Group's
PowerKids Press
New York

Published in 1996 by The Rosen Publishing Group, Inc.
29 East 21st Street, New York, NY 10010

First Edition

Photo credits: Cover photo © Bill Aron; pp. 4, 15 © Jack Kurtz/Impact Visuals; p. 7 © Donna Binder/Impact Visuals; pp. 8, 11 © Jeffrey D. Scott/Impact Visuals; p. 12 © Michelle & Tom Grimm/International Stock; p. 16 © Donna De Cesare/Impact Visuals; p. 19 © Abu Hander/International Stock; p. 20 © Sharon Stewart/Impact Visuals.

Book Design and Layout: Erin McKenna and Kim Sonsky

Chalfonte, Jessica.
    I am Muslim / Jessica Chalfonte. — 1st ed.
       p.   cm. — (Religions of the world)
    Includes Index.
    Summary: Introduces the fundamentals of Islam through the eyes of a Muslim child living in Detroit.
    ISBN 0-8239-2375-4
    1. Islam—Juvenile literature. [1. Islam.] I. Title. II. Series: Religions of the world (Rosen Publishing Group)
BPI61.2.C45 1996
297—dc20
                                 96-732
                                 CIP
                                 AC

Contents

Islam

My name is Ahmet. I live in Detroit. I am Muslim. That means that I practice the religion of Islam. Muslims live in many different countries and cultures. The word Islam means "**submission** (sub-MISH-un) to God." Being a Muslim means following a way of life every day in order to please God. We pray five times a day. When we pray, we take off our shoes and kneel toward Mecca, a holy city in Saudi Arabia.

◄ Muslims must pray five times a day.

Allah

The word for God in Arabic, the language of our religion, is Allah. My mother and father have taught me that nothing can be compared to Allah. Allah is different from all people and all things. Nothing is like Allah. We believe that Allah knows all things, can do all things, and has always existed. Everything exists because Allah wills, or wants, it to exist.

In some cities, special parades are held to celebrate Islam. ▶

Muhammad

We believe that a man named Muhammad was one of Allah's **prophets** (PRAH-fits). Muslims call him the Great Prophet and the Chosen Messenger. The book about how Allah wants us to live our lives was **revealed** (re-VEELD) to Muhammad in Arabic. This book is called the **Qur'an** (kor-ON). It was written in Arabic. Muhammad taught us that there is only one Allah.

Muslims believe that Muhammad received the Islamic holy book, the Qur'an, from Allah's angel.

The Qur'an

We believe that Muhammad received the Qur'an from Allah's angel. We believe that the Qur'an came from Allah. My family reads the Qur'an often. We study it so that we can understand how Allah expects us to behave. My father says that the Qur'an was written in heaven before Allah created all things.

It is important for Muslims to study the Qur'an. ▶

Mosque

My family goes to a **mosque** (MOSK) to pray and to learn about our faith. Muslim religious leaders, called **imams** (ee-MOMZ), teach us. Every mosque has a tower called a **minaret** (min-are-RET). Five times a day, a **muezzin** (moo-ez-ZEN) calls us to prayer from the tower.

◀ *A mosque is a Muslim house of worship.*

Islamic Law

Islamic law is called **Shari'a** (shar-ee-AH). It is based on the Qur'an. Shari'a helps us understand how to practice our religion in our daily lives. Sometimes my father or his friends ask our imams to explain the law and how we should understand it.

There are five main duties or **pillars** (PIL-lars) in Islam. The first pillar of a Muslim is to recite the **Shahada** (sha-HAH-da), or confession of faith. My mother and father taught me the Shahada.

Many Muslims study the Qur'an together. ▶

Prayer

A second pillar is to pray correctly. We believe that an angel showed Muhammad how to pray. All Muslims pray in the same way. First, we remove our shoes. We wash our hands and face and feet. We kneel down on a clean spot on the ground or on a mat. When we pray, we face toward Mecca. We pray five times a day: at dawn, in the middle of the day, in the afternoon, after sunset, and before going to bed.

◀ *Muslims face the holy city of Mecca each time they pray.*

The Hajj

A third pillar is the **Hajj** (HODGE), a journey to the holy city of Mecca. Every Muslim *must* try to make the Hajj at least once in his or her life.

During the Hajj, people say prayers and listen to sermons. There are special activities that everyone does together. In Mecca is the Ka'ba, the sacred cube building. It is the most sacred and holy place in Islam.

I look forward to the day that I can make the Hajj with my family.

Making the Hajj is one of the most important events in a Muslim's life. ▶

Ramadan

A fourth pillar is the **observance** (ob-ZER-vents) of Ramadan. Ramadan is a month in the Islamic calendar. In this month, we fast from dawn to sunset. This means that adults and older kids do not eat all day. I do not have to fast like my parents and sisters because I am still young. During Ramadan, we remember our duty to God. At the end of the month, we have a great feast. It is called **'Idu l-Fitr** (EE-du el-FEE-tra), the festival of breaking the fast.

'Idu l-Fitr, at the end of Ramadan, is a joyous festival.

Almsgiving

A fifth pillar is giving alms, or charity to the poor. The giving of charity is a very important part of being a good Muslim. It is called Zakat. The Qur'an teaches us to give to the poor, the needy, and to travelers. My mother and I also help needy people and charities as well.

Glossary

Hajj (HODGE) Journey to Mecca.

'Idu l-Fitr (EE-du el-FEE-tra) Festival at the end of Ramadan.

imam (ee-MOM) Religious leader.

minaret (min-are-RET) Tower on a mosque.

mosque (MOSK) Place where Muslims pray.

muezzin (moo-ez-ZEN) Person who calls Muslims to pray.

observe (ob-ZERV) Recognize a holy day.

pillars (PIL-lars) Religious duties.

prophet (PRAH-fit) Messenger from God.

Qur'an (kor-ON) The Islamic holy book.

reveal (re-VEEL) Make known.

Shahada (sha-HAH-da) Muslim confession of faith.

Shari'a (shar-ee-AH) Islamic law.

submission (sub-MISH-un) Obeying someone else.

Index